Find One Cocktail Without a Copy

Find One Ice cream Without a Copy

Find One Crocodile Without a Copy

Find One Flamingo Without a Copy

Find One Monkey Without a Copy

Find One Picture Without a Copy

Find One Picture Without a Copy

Find One Picture Without a Copy

Find One Picture Without a Copy

Find One Picture Without a Copy

Find One Picture Without a Copy

Find One Picture Without a Copy

Find One Picture Without a Copy

Find One Picture Without a Copy

Find One Picture Without a Copy

Find One Picture Without a Copy

Find One Picture Without a Copy

Find One Picture Without a Copy

Find One Picture Without a Copy

Find One Picture Without a Copy

Find One Picture Without a Copy

Find One Picture Without a Copy

Find One Picture Without a Copy

Find One Picture Without a Copy

Find One Picture Without a Copy

Find One Picture Without a Copy

Find One Picture Without a Copy

Find One Picture Without a Copy

Find One Picture Without a Copy

Find One Picture Without a Copy

Find One Picture Without a Copy

Find One Picture Without a Copy

Find One Picture Without a Copy

Find One Picture Without a Copy

Find Two Identical pictures of Colorful Balloons.

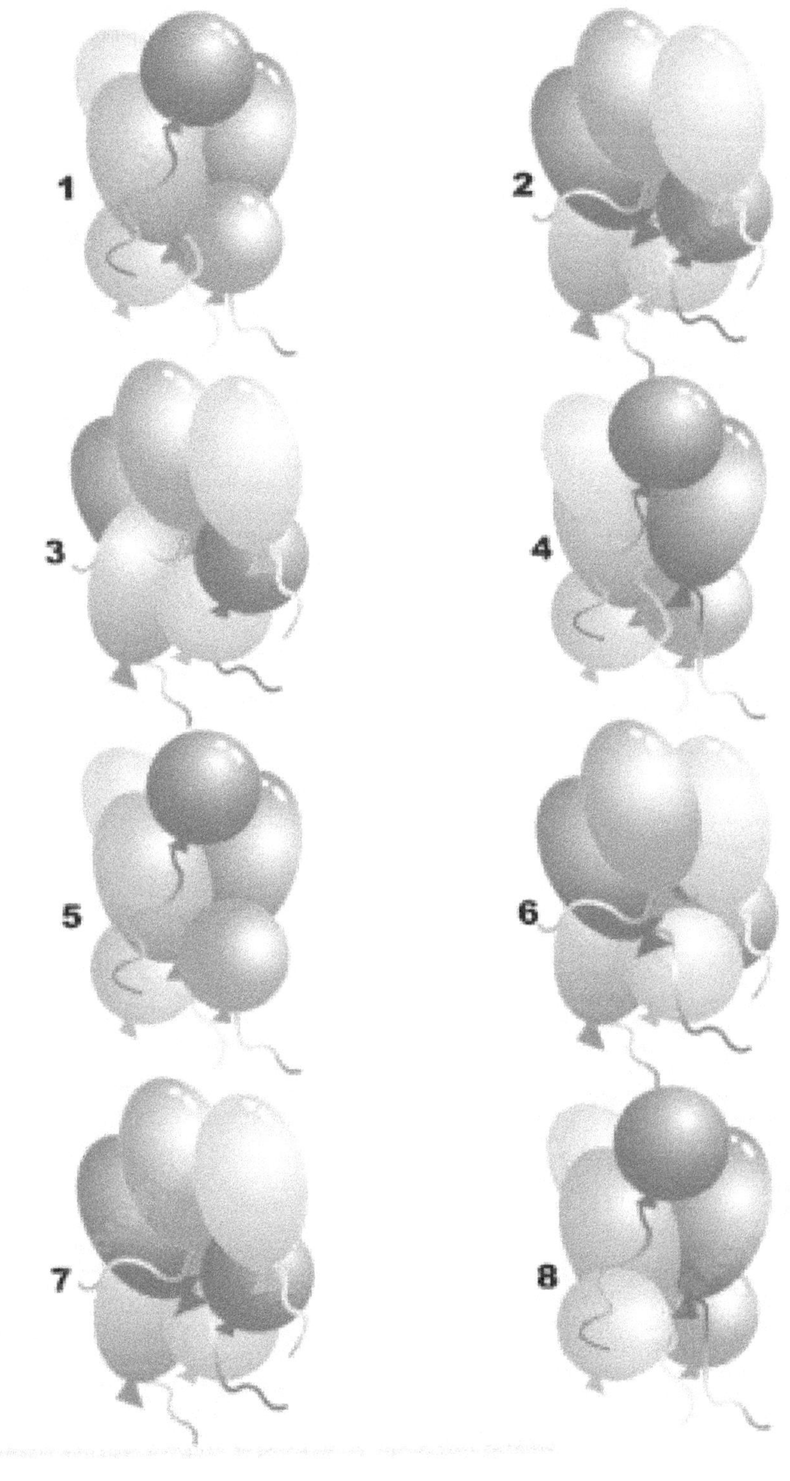

Find Two Identical pictures of Reptiles.

Find Two Identical pictures of Parrots.

Find Two Identical pictures of Ocean Animals.

Find Two Identical pictures of Mice.

Find Two Identical pictures of Mammals.

Find Two Identical pictures of Farm Animals.

Find Two Identical pictures of Dogs.

Find Two Identical pictures of Cars.

Find Two Identical pictures of Cute Bears.

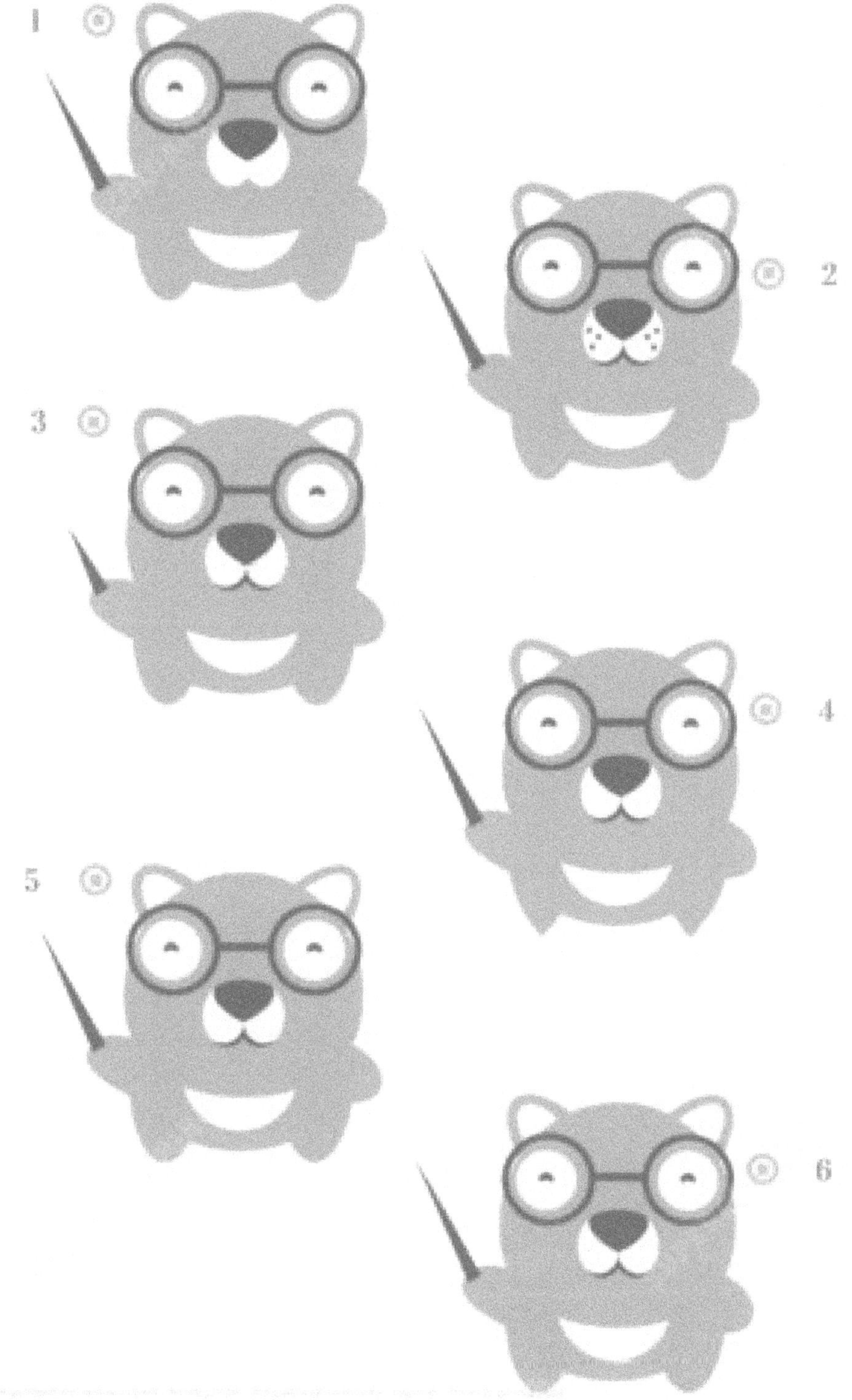

Find Two Identical pictures of Cute Elephants.

Find Two Identical pictures of Cute Monkeys.

Find Two Identical pictures of Turtles.